Contents

Words shown in **bold** in the text are explained in the glossary.

All the places in this book are shown on the map on page 22.

Off to School

It's morning, and all over the world millions of children are waking up, getting dressed and heading off to school.

These girls are walking to school in India.

In the United States and Canada, children ride to school on yellow buses.

These students in Myanmar travel to and from school by boat.

This small and overcrowded bus is carrying children to school in Indonesia.

5

Our Classrooms

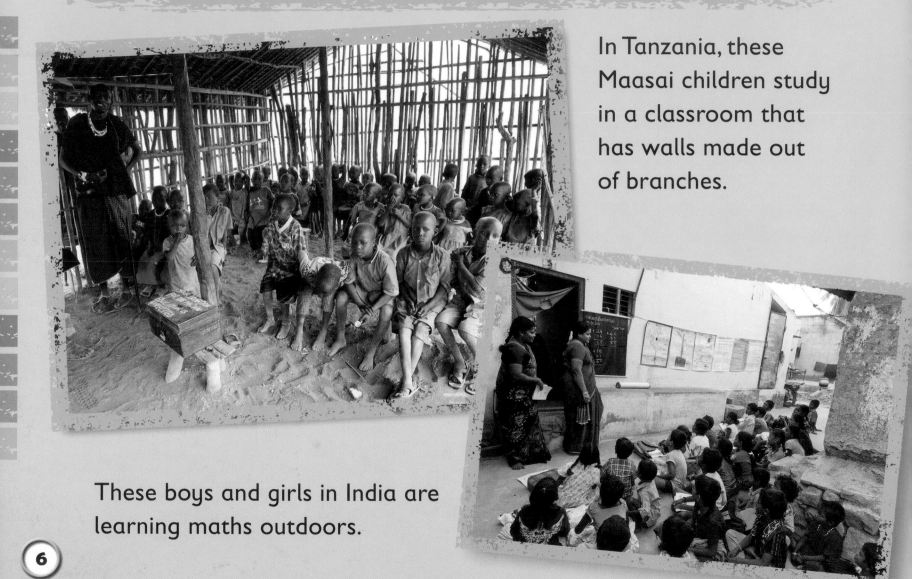

In Tanzania, these Maasai children study in a classroom that has walls made out of branches.

These boys and girls in India are learning maths outdoors.

This classroom in Russia is decorated with balloons for the first day of term in September. On this day, children bring flowers for their teachers and wear their best clothes.

A Very Tiny School

The Scottish island of Canna is home to one of the smallest schools in the world.

Only a few families live on Canna.

So sometimes Canna School has just three or four pupils!

A farmhouse on Canna

Once children on Canna are 12 years old, they go to school on the mainland. The **ferry** journey can take nearly three hours. So children live at the school and only go home for the weekend every two weeks.

This photo shows four pupils and a teacher at Canna School.

SCHOOL

The school building

What Do We Do at School?

We read and write and study maths and science.

These Xingu children in the Amazon rainforest are reading.

Some children work on computers and tablets.

This girl in India does her schoolwork on a chalkboard.

We have fun making art.

These kids on the Falkland Islands have painted pictures of large seabirds called albatrosses. The birds come to the islands to lay eggs and raise their chicks.

We sing, make music and dance.

We see our friends and favourite teachers.

The Camel Library

It's fun to go to the library to choose a book. Imagine, though, if the library came to you on the back of a camel!

The camel library

In Kenya, many people are **nomads** who move from place to place with their animals.

Their small villages, or camps, are usually far from towns.

So a camel library visits the nomads' villages.

The camel library visits a school for nomad children.

A librarian and a camel herder travel with three camels. The animals carry about 200 books between them.

Earthquake Drills

Japan is a country that has many **earthquakes**.

An earthquake can cause terrible damage to buildings.

Most Japanese schools have an earthquake drill once a month.

This teaches children what to do if an earthquake happens.

Children practise hiding under their desks to stay safe from falling walls or ceilings.

Japanese children hiding under desks

Buildings that are damaged by an earthquake may catch fire. During an earthquake drill, children wear fireproof hoods and practise taking different escape routes from their school.

Learning on Class Trips

Lots of learning goes on outside the classroom.

These children in Scotland are on a class trip to learn about life on a farm.

An elephant keeper

A two-month-old
elephant calf

These schoolchildren in Kenya are visiting a
centre for baby elephants that have lost their mothers.

The mother elephants were killed by hunters called **poachers**.

At the centre, children learn about protecting elephants.

A School in a Tent

In 2011, a war began in Syria.

Millions of Syrian people left their homes to escape from danger.

Many people found safety at the Al Zaatari **refugee** camp in Jordan.

At the camp, some children go to school in tent classrooms.

A teacher at the camp rings the bell for school to start.

A tent classroom

On school days, children leave their tent homes. Then they walk through the large camp to their school. Girls have their lessons in the morning and boys go to school in the afternoon.

19

No Time for School

Many children cannot go to school because they have to work.

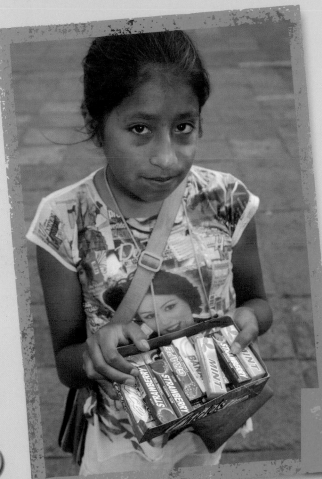

This girl in Peru earns money selling chewing gum on the street.

They must help their families pay for food and medical care.

Thankfully, many people are trying to help working children.

One thing that can be changed is to make bosses pay adult workers higher wages.

If parents can earn more money, their children won't have to work.

In Cambodia, some children work on filthy, smelly rubbish dumps. They collect plastic to sell to recycling companies. The children earn just a few pence for a whole day's work.

21

Where in the World?

Canada
Page 10

United States
Page 5

Canna, Scotland
Pages 8–9

Scotland
Page 16

Germany
Page 11

India
Pages 4, 6 and 10

China
Front cover

Russia
Page 7

Canada
Page 10

Haiti
Page 11

North America

Europe

Asia

Japan
Pages 14–15

Jordan
Pages 18–19

Africa

Cambodia
Page 21

South America

Tanzania
Page 6

Australia

Brazil
Page 10

Peru
Page 20

Falkland Islands
Page 11

Kenya
Pages 12–13 and 17

Myanmar
Page 5

Indonesia
Page 5

Glossary

earthquake
A sudden shaking caused by underground movements in Earth's outer layer, or crust.

ferry
A boat that regularly carries people or vehicles from one place to another. A ferry is a little like a bus, except that it carries people over water instead of land.

nomad
A person who regularly moves from one area to another and does not live in one place all the time.

poacher
A person who breaks the law by killing an animal or taking it from its natural habitat.

refugee
A person who has been forced to leave his or her home to escape danger and needs to be protected.

Index

Learn More Online

To learn more about schools around the world, go to
www.rubytuesdaybooks.com/school